Healing Miracles in Acts of the Apostles

Healing Miracles in Acts of the Apostles

PAUL FEIDER

RESOURCE *Publications* • Eugene, Oregon

HEALING MIRACLES IN ACTS OF THE APOSTLES

Copyright © 2021 Paul Feider. All rights reserved. Except for brief quotations in critical publications or reviews, no part of this book may be reproduced in any manner without prior written permission from the publisher. Write: Permissions, Wipf and Stock Publishers, 199 W. 8th Ave., Suite 3, Eugene, OR 97401.

Resource Publications
An Imprint of Wipf and Stock Publishers
199 W. 8th Ave., Suite 3
Eugene, OR 97401

www.wipfandstock.com

PAPERBACK ISBN: 978-1-6667-0265-1
HARDCOVER ISBN: 978-1-6667-0266-8
EBOOK ISBN: 978-1-6667-0267-5

06/25/21

Scriptures taken from *The Holy Bible,* New International Version, NIV Copyright 1973, 1978, 1984, 2011 by Biblica, Inc. All rights reserved worldwide.

Thank you Jamie Ferger, Donna Self, Laura Sinclair and Vickie Bauch for your help in editing this book.

Contents

Layout of this Book | ix
Introduction | xi

Session 1: The Miracle of Remaining Together | 1
Session 2: The Outpouring of the Holy Spirit | 6
Session 3: The Miracle of *Metanoia* | 11
Session 4: The Healing of the Crippled Man | 15
Session 5: Self-Assurance with the Holy Spirit | 19
Session 6: Many People Were Cured | 24
Session 7: The Anointing of Deacons | 28
Session 8: The Miracle of Stephen | 32
Session 9: Miracles in Samaria | 36
Session 10: The Miraculous Encounter | 41
Session 11: Miracles in Lydda and Joppa | 46
Session 12: The Miracle of Cornelius | 51
Session 13: Miracles in Antioch | 56
Session 14: Healings in Lystra | 61
Session 15: Healings in Philippi | 66
Session 16: Miracles in Ephesus | 72
Session 17: The Raising of Eutychus | 77
Session 18: Healings in Malta | 82

Recommmended Reading | 87

Layout of this Book

To receive the most from this book we begin each session with a *prayer for openness* to the message God has for us. Invite God's love and wisdom to permeate your heart and mind as you read these miracle-filled accounts in Acts of the Apostles.

Each session in this book will give several verses that focus on one healing or transforming event recorded in Acts. Following those verses is a *reflection*.

Following the reflection are *questions for reflection/discussion*. This book can be completed individually, but there are greater benefits if shared with a group.

If you have a group, you are encouraged to *pray after the session with each other* for any areas that need healing or a greater outpouring of the Holy Spirit.

The final part of this series is *Practical Applications*. These are meant to assist in making real changes in our lives because of our journey into Acts of the Apostles.

Introduction

Many have studied the miracles in the gospels and discovered the power of Jesus' love to change lives and draw people into a saving faith relationship with him. He was filled with the perfect love of the Father. He carried that love to every person he encountered. This perfect love, which is called *agape* in the New Testament, brought about physical, emotional and spiritual healing as well as dispelled evil. He taught his disciples that they could receive that love from the Father and be empowered to heal others.

In this book we will explore 18 of the healing and transforming miracles in Acts of the Apostles. We will read how the love of the Father that overflowed in Jesus was poured out on the disciples after the resurrection which empowered them to experience healing and to minister healing to others. Acts of the Apostles demonstrates that people like us can receive this love, this Holy Spirit, and do the things that Jesus did. As followers of Jesus we are commissioned to continue manifesting this healing energy by living in the presence of the Father's love.

As we step into the Acts of the Apostles, we will discover what was at the heart of the early Christian communities. We can uncover what gave these first Christians the power to heal, emboldened them to stay with Jesus' message in the face of persecution and empowered them to overcome differences and live as a community. These first disciples were not just trying to get to heaven, although we can believe that they did; they were actively bringing heaven to earth. They were proclaiming the risen presence of Jesus

Introduction

in word and action. They formed the first healing communities and their story offers us a challenging and yet compelling picture of how to live in the power of the Holy Spirit.

In these accounts, we see how people like us changed the world in which they lived and did it as a normal part of their commitment to Jesus. These were ordinary people doing extraordinary things because they submitted to the extraordinary power of the Holy Spirit. These stories were written not just to tell us about Jesus and his followers but to change us to become like him and those we call disciples. We can hardly read Acts of the Apostles and not wonder what it was like to walk in the sandals of those early believers and to see the demonstrations of power manifested by those anointed with the full energy of the Holy Spirit. We invite that anointing to fill us as we make this journey into these stories.

BACKGROUND TO ACTS OF THE APOSTLES

Acts of the Apostles was written by Luke, who also wrote the Gospel of Luke. He seems to have known the Apostles, Mary, Paul, and many of the early disciples. Toward the end of Acts, we read evidence that Luke traveled with Paul and witnessed the miraculous power of the Holy Spirit. His Gospel and Acts preserve for us a complete account of the life of Jesus and the early church community. He portrays a great awareness of the miracles of Jesus and the Holy Spirit's presence after the resurrection, which empowered the early disciples to do the type of miracles that Jesus did. In his book, *The Gospel of the Holy Spirit*, Alfred McBride writes, "Scarcely a paragraph or page goes by without a reference to the dynamic presence of the Spirit in the lives of the people who carry Jesus to the world. Every new development, every distinct growth is linked with its divine origin."

Acts of the Apostles gives us an inspiring picture of those early disciples. They preached, built community, healed, spoke in tongues, discerned, loved, taught, and died for their belief, and all of this was not seen as unusual but quite normal.

Introduction

This journey into Acts will allow us to witness the miraculous power of the Holy Spirit in the lives of people like us. *That same power is available to us today!* This book tells us how to access that power, that anointing, so that we might bring healing and the fullness of life to those we meet.

PURPOSE OF THIS BOOK

The purpose of this book is to introduce us to the full anointing of the Holy Spirit as it existed in the early Christian community. It is meant to encourage, yes, even compel us to accept fully the gift of the Holy Spirit so that we might be changed as well as change those around us.

FURTHER RESOURCES

If you find this book to be helpful for you, you may wish to check out other resources on healing and the power of the Holy Spirit. The Order of St. Luke (OSL) is a community of Christians who pray with people for healing by the power of the Holy Spirit and train people who wish to do the same. This community consists of almost 200 Healing Communities around the country and a number of virtual Healing Communities, all of which pray together and reach out to pray with others for physical, emotional, and spiritual healing. To get more information about this organization, visit our website at www.OSLToday.org. You can also find many more videos and books about healing and the transforming energy of the Holy Spirit there.

One powerful series, which is the introduction for OSL membership, is the study of the *26 Miracles of Jesus*. It is a video series with a discussion book. People have been transformed as they discover the power of Jesus' love that brought healing to so many. Often, they want to then participate in his healing ministry themselves.

Introduction

The Spiritual Enrichment Seminars referred to in this book is available through *www.OSLToday.org*. It is a six-session series inviting people to experience the full power of the Holy Spirit.

The OSL office is:
P.O. Box 780909
San Antonio, TX 78278-909
Phone: (210) 492-5222

SESSION 1

The Miracle of Remaining Together

PRAYER FOR OPENNESS

(This, or a prayer like it, could be used to begin every session.)

Jesus, open my mind and my heart to your message in these scriptures as I read them and reflect on their meaning for me. Anoint me with an awareness of your loving presence and the power of your Holy Spirit as I ponder these stories and seek to immerse myself more fully in your word. Enlighten me to the meaning of these accounts for my life and ministry today. Fill me with the courage to live out the challenges of being your disciple. Send the fullness of your Spirit upon me as I make this journey into Acts of the Apostles that I might be empowered to live your mission in my life. Amen.

READ ACTS 1:1–9

¹In my former book, Theophilus, I wrote about all that Jesus began to do and to teach ²until the day he was taken up to heaven, after giving instructions through the Holy Spirit to the apostles he had chosen. ³After his suffering, he presented himself to them and gave many convincing proofs that he was alive. He appeared to them over a period of forty days and spoke about the kingdom

of God. ⁴On one occasion, while he was eating with them, he gave them this command: "Do not leave Jerusalem, but wait for the gift my Father promised, which you have heard me speak about. ⁵For John baptized with water, but in a few days, you will be baptized with the Holy Spirit."

⁶Then they gathered around him and asked him, "Lord, are you at this time going to restore the kingdom to Israel?"

⁷He said to them: "It is not for you to know the times or dates the Father has set by his own authority. ⁸But you will receive power when the Holy Spirit comes on you; and you will be my witnesses in Jerusalem, and in all Judea and Samaria, and to the ends of the earth."

⁹After he said this, he was taken up before their very eyes, and a cloud hid him from their sight.

ACTS 1:14-17

¹⁴They all joined together constantly in prayer, along with the women and Mary the mother of Jesus, and with his brothers.

¹⁵In those days Peter stood up among the believers (a group numbering about a hundred and twenty) ¹⁶and said, "Brothers and sisters, the Scripture had to be fulfilled in which the Holy Spirit spoke long ago through David concerning Judas, who served as guide for those who arrested Jesus. ¹⁷He was one of our number and shared in our ministry."

ACTS 1:21-26

²¹Therefore it is necessary to choose one of the men who have been with us the whole time the Lord Jesus was living among us, ²²beginning from John's baptism to the time when Jesus was taken up from us. For one of these must become a witness with us of his resurrection."

²³So they nominated two men: Joseph called Barsabbas (also known as Justus) and Matthias. ²⁴Then they prayed, "Lord, you

The Miracle of Remaining Together

know everyone's heart. Show us which of these two you have chosen ²⁵to take over this apostolic ministry, which Judas left to go where he belongs." ²⁶Then they cast lots, and the lot fell to Matthias; so he was added to the eleven apostles.

REFLECTION

As we begin this journey into the miracles in Acts, we might consider what healings had to happen for this group of disciples to stay together. They were very different and somehow had to move past their differences if they were going to continue Jesus' important mission of bringing the fullness of life. In other cases, at this time, where a person tried to lead a movement but then got killed, the disciples scattered, and the movement ended (Acts 5:36-37). Jesus' disciples remained together and prayed. They did what they often saw the Master do (Mark 1:35; Luke 5:16; Luke 11:1-4). They obediently waited for the empowerment that Jesus promised. Together, they had to heal through grief at losing a friend, anger at those who killed him, guilt about deserting him in the garden, and fear about what would happen to them now. They needed "inner healing". They had to take time to feel the peace of Jesus which he offered to them when he appeared after his resurrection. They had to empty themselves of all inner distractions and to forgive so that they could be filled with this outpouring of the Holy Spirit of which Jesus spoke.

    I once was assigned as pastor of a community that had gone through a scandal with the former pastor. Many people were hurt and angry. I began by praying with the people for inner healing, and I spoke of their need to forgive. We celebrated a community healing service and I invited people to release their hurts to Jesus and receive his deep love. Soon after I led the Spiritual Enrichment Seminars. (This is a six-session series I developed with reflections and daily meditations inviting people to feel God's deep love for them and then pray for a fresh outpouring of God's Holy Spirit.) Many people experienced God's personal love for them and new energy for ministry. Soon they wanted to learn more about

Healing Miracles in Acts of the Apostles

scripture and go out to bring healing to others. The effects of the former events were gone, and they became a healing community. They felt called to continue Jesus' mission just as this early community of Christians did.

The first Christians desired to carry on Jesus' work, but they had no clear plan to accomplish that. They had to listen and discern how Jesus might wish them to carry on his ministry. They discerned the need to choose another apostle to fill Judas' place. The candidate's criteria were that this person would know the heart and mind of Jesus by walking with Jesus from his baptism to the ascension. They used a method which they felt allowed the Holy Spirit to guide the process. All of this they did as a community while they waited in prayer. It was a great miracle that they experienced inner healing and remained together. This miracle made other miracles possible.

QUESTIONS FOR REFLECTION/DISCUSSION

1. What do you hope to receive from this journey into the Healing Miracles in Acts?

2. How have you experienced the gift of being together with other disciples?

3. What people do you think could help you open yourself to the awesome, transforming power of God's love?

4. What thoughts or feelings would you need to release into Jesus' hands to ready yourself for a greater infusion of the Holy Spirit? Who could help you?

5. What do you think of their method of choosing another apostle? How might that be incorporated today in choosing Christian leaders?

6. What decisions and encounters have you seen in this first session that you might apply to your own life and community?

TIME OF PRAYER WITH EACH OTHER

PRACTICAL APPLICATION

In order to prepare for greater infusion of the Holy Spirit, ask God to show you what feelings (such as grief, anger, hurt, or fear) seem to be unresolved or keeping your life from being well. When you are ready, ask someone to pray with you for inner healing.

SESSION 2

The Outpouring of the Holy Spirit

PRAYER

READ ACTS 2:1-12

When the day of Pentecost came, they were all together in one place. ²Suddenly a sound like the blowing of a violent wind came from heaven and filled the whole house where they were sitting. ³They saw what seemed to be tongues of fire that separated and came to rest on each of them. ⁴All of them were filled with the Holy Spirit and began to speak in other tongues as the Spirit enabled them.

⁵Now there were staying in Jerusalem God-fearing Jews from every nation under heaven. ⁶When they heard this sound, a crowd came together in bewilderment, because each one heard their own language being spoken. ⁷Utterly amazed, they asked: "Aren't all these who are speaking Galileans? ⁸Then how is it that each of us hears them in our native language? ⁹Parthians, Medes and Elamites; residents of Mesopotamia, Judea and Cappadocia, Pontus and Asia, ¹⁰Phrygia and Pamphylia, Egypt and the parts of Libya near Cyrene; visitors from Rome ¹¹(both Jews and converts to Judaism); Cretans and Arabs—we hear them declaring the

wonders of God in our own tongues!" ¹²Amazed and perplexed, they asked one another, "What does this mean?"

REFLECTION

This account tells of a miraculous event that happened during the Pentecost celebration. This early group of disciples experienced something incredible. Jesus had promised to send his Spirit, but I doubt if they could have imagined what that would be like. They heard the wind, they saw tongues of fire, and started to speak in tongues which they did not know. People of various languages could understand them. Even more extraordinary is that they were emboldened to speak of Jesus without fear. When we read of the reaction of those who witnessed this event, it is clear that God was moving, heaven was coming to earth, barriers were breaking down. The people were seeing something they had never seen before. The disciples experienced a new power, a new courage. Jesus' mission was going to continue, empowered by the Holy Spirit.

I remember once we were leading a healing Eucharist in the cathedral in the capital of Holland. About 700 people packed the cathedral for this service. As I gave the sermon, I could feel the heaviness among the people. It felt like a sadness. When I finished preaching, instead of asking the people to stand together to proclaim the creed, I invited people to pray quietly, and when they felt ready, to make a new, personal commitment to Jesus as Lord of their life. As a sign that they had made that commitment, they were to stand. For quite a while, no one stood. All of a sudden, one stood and then another. One by one, each person stood. Then, to my amazement, the whole group started singing in tongues. It was a thing of divine beauty. The whole gothic cathedral was filled with God-given song in multiple harmonies. Once it subsided, the heaviness had lifted, and people were ready to celebrate the Eucharist. Many received healings during that service. That, however, was not the end of the story.

After the service, when I was in the sacristy removing my vestment, a man stood at the door and asked, "Do you know what they were singing at that one point in the service?" The other speaker tried to explain that when people pray in tongues, we do not understand it but that the Holy Spirit is simply praying through them (Rom 8:26–27). "No," he said, "Do you know what they were saying? They were praying the prayers that the Jews pray at the Wailing Wall." He was Jewish and understood the words during the singing in tongues! The Spirit had prayed through these people to lift their heaviness and open them to healing. I was blown away. It was an awesome sign of God's presence.

At the Pentecost event, the disciples experienced something within themselves that brought about significant changes. Their grief, anger, and fear were healed as they experienced this outpouring of the Holy Spirit. This was a heart experience. This was an influx of perfect love as if Jesus was right there with them. Their speech was beyond words. All could understand that they were talking about eternal things. These regular people were anointed to do God's mission on earth. It was a miracle.

I have had an experience like this, and I have seen many people receive this infusion of God's love empowering them for ministry. Often it happens as part of the Spiritual Enrichment Seminars, but it also occurs in private prayer or during times of worship. The disciples waited in prayer, expecting the Spirit to be poured out. Prayer and expectancy set the stage for this divine anointing.

QUESTIONS FOR REFLECTION/DISCUSSION

1. What did the disciples do to prepare themselves for this outpouring of the Holy Spirit?

2. The disciples knew Jesus, but they needed to wait for another baptism, which would empower them for ministry. Have you

The Outpouring of the Holy Spirit

ever taken time to prepare and pray for a baptism of empowerment, to feel God's deep love in your heart? Are you willing to try it?

3. This empowerment baptism or baptism of the Holy Spirit was a normal part of the early Christian life. Why do you think churches lost it? Who could help revive it?

4. How do you think churches would be different if every person took time to receive inner healing and the empowerment of the Holy Spirit?

5. I felt the heaviness lift off of the people in the cathedral when they sang in tongues. Have you ever had an experience similar to that? Share.

6. What insight about living the Christian life did you receive from this session?

TIME OF PRAYER WITH EACH OTHER

PRACTICAL APPLICATION

Talk with people in your community about this empowerment baptism. Have they received it? Ask them to tell you about it. Share your experience.

PRAYER TO RECEIVE THE FULL ANOINTING OF THE HOLY SPIRIT

Father, I thank you for sending Jesus to show us your love and promise us the fullness of life found in the power of your Holy Spirit. Jesus, I now ask for the infusion of your Spirit into my life. I repent of anything in my life that is not in accord with your will, and I ask for your mercy to cleanse me. I pray your healing love to flow through my life story and release any feelings that hinder me from living fully for you. I declare my deep desire to experience a fuller outpouring of your Holy Spirit and I open myself to all the gifts of your Spirit. Jesus, I ask your Spirit to empower me the way that your Spirit empowered the first disciples at Pentecost. I want you from now on to be Lord of my life. Thank you for loving me and hearing me. Amen.

SESSION 3

The Miracle of *Metanoia*

PRAYER

READ ACTS 2:37-47

(Acts 2:14-36 gives the context of Peter's speech)
⁣ ³⁷When the people heard this, they were cut to the heart and said to Peter and the other apostles, "Brothers, what shall we do?"
⁣ ³⁸Peter replied, "Repent and be baptized, every one of you, in the name of Jesus Christ for the forgiveness of your sins. And you will receive the gift of the Holy Spirit. ³⁹The promise is for you and your children and for all who are far off—for all whom the Lord our God will call."
⁣ ⁴⁰With many other words he warned them; and he pleaded with them, "Save yourselves from this corrupt generation." ⁴¹Those who accepted his message were baptized, and about three thousand were added to their number that day.
⁣ ⁴²They devoted themselves to the apostles teaching and to fellowship, to the breaking of bread and to prayer. ⁴³Everyone was filled with awe at the many wonders and signs performed by the apostles. ⁴⁴All the believers were together and had everything in common. ⁴⁵They sold property and possessions to give to anyone

who had need. ⁴⁶Every day they continued to meet together in the temple courts. They broke bread in their homes and ate together with glad and sincere hearts, ⁴⁷praising God and enjoying the favor of all the people. And the Lord added to their number daily those who were being saved.

REFLECTION

After the Pentecost event, the compelling speech of Peter led to the important question of the hearers, namely, "What must we do?" Whatever they saw and whatever they heard made many bystanders ask, "What must we do to get what you have?" This attitude of openness gave room for Peter to offer them the challenge. He said, "You must *metanoia*; that is, you must reform; you must turn around." (*Metanoia* is the Greek word meaning repent or change direction.) He was saying to them that they had to turn around and go in a different direction. With such a challenge, it is a miracle that 3000 people came forth to be baptized that day. If we desire to let our life be guided by the voice of Jesus and receive his power, we must turn away from activities not consistent with his teaching and surrender our will to his. We must empty ourselves of the old way of doing things and begin patterning our life on that of Jesus. We must be directed from "above" (See John 3:3) instead of just doing our own will. Peter is saying that this *metanoia* is necessary to receive the power of the Holy Spirit through baptism. It prepares our heart and mind and soul for the infusion of the Holy Spirit.

This *metanoia* often means repenting of past wrongs, emptying old thoughts and feelings, and opening to be filled with the full anointing of the Holy Spirit. It is a letting go of my will and anything incompatible with the message of Jesus. It is a surrender into the will of God, to listen for divine direction in life choices. This may seem quite challenging and even scary to let go of control, but it brings a deep peace letting our Creator guide our lives. It is living our life in the Spirit, empowered to handle whatever comes along.

The Miracle of Metanoia

The last five verses of this section describe how the early Christians lived in the Holy Spirit and how they continued to nurture their new-found life through teachings, community life, breaking of the bread or Holy Communion, and the prayers. They turned from a human way of thinking to a God-directed and empowered way of living. They became a divine-led community, listening in prayer, receiving Eucharist, learning together, and sharing their resources as they were directed. They were willing to stand together through the challenges that they would face because the mission demanded it and because the Spirit empowered it. They were a healing community.

We may not be called to live in community exactly as they did. Still, by receiving God-directed teaching, sharing weekly worship and Communion, taking time for personal prayer and sharing our resources with others, we keep our life in the Spirit vibrant and growing. This life is available to all who choose it. It is a life of true inner peace and joy.

QUESTIONS FOR REFLECTION/DISCUSSION

1. What do you think it was that moved Peter's hearers to ask their question, "What must we do?"

2. What answer do you think those in the crowd were expecting from Peter?

3. We all have a sense of wanting to control our lives. What would it mean for you to let God control your life? Does it feel scary?

Healing Miracles in Acts of the Apostles

4. How is your Christian church or community like that described in verses 42–47?

5. What can you do to help your church or community become more like the early Christian community? What parts of that would you like to model? What *metanoia* would have to happen?

6. What comes to mind when you read that in order to receive Jesus' power, you may need to turn away from activities not consistent with his teaching and surrender your will to his?

TIME OF PRAYER WITH EACH OTHER

PRACTICAL APPLICATION

Ask God to show you what you might have to turn away from to live a full life in the Spirit. Talk with a trusted person about what might change, and how to go about it.

SESSION 4

The Healing of the Crippled Man

PRAYER

READ ACTS 3:1-12

One day Peter and John were going up to the temple at the time of prayer—at three in the afternoon. ²Now a man who was lame from birth was being carried to the temple gate called Beautiful, where he was put every day to beg from those going into the temple courts. ³When he saw Peter and John about to enter, he asked them for money. ⁴Peter looked straight at him, as did John. Then Peter said, "Look at us!" ⁵So the man gave them his attention, expecting to get something from them.

⁶Then Peter said, "Silver or gold I do not have, but what I do have I give you. In the name of Jesus Christ of Nazareth, walk." ⁷Taking him by the right hand, he helped him up, and instantly the man's feet and ankles became strong. ⁸He jumped to his feet and began to walk. Then he went with them into the temple courts, walking and jumping, and praising God. ⁹When all the people saw him walking and praising God, ¹⁰they recognized him as the same man who used to sit begging at the temple gate called Beautiful,

and they were filled with wonder and amazement at what had happened to him.

¹¹While the man held on to Peter and John, all the people were astonished and came running to them in the place called Solomon's Colonnade. ¹²When Peter saw this, he said to them: "Fellow Israelites, why does this surprise you? Why do you stare at us as if by our own power or godliness we had made this man walk?

ACTS 3:15-16

¹⁵"You killed the author of life, but God raised him from the dead. We are witnesses of this. ¹⁶By faith in the name of Jesus, this man whom you see and know was made strong. It is Jesus' name and the faith that comes through him that has completely healed him, as you can all see."

REFLECTION

Since Jesus was the Son of God, we might understand how he could cure people as recorded in the gospels, but here we read of a person like us bringing the healing power of Jesus to another person. Peter says, "In the name of Jesus Christ, walk." He is saying, by the power of the person of Jesus, you can walk. The man is only asking for money and probably did not know Jesus, but Peter brings Jesus to this encounter through his deep, committed connection to Jesus. We read in verse 16 that Peter had a deep faith relationship with Jesus, which allowed the crippled man to experience the power of Jesus' love at that moment. It is the experience of Jesus' intense love that brings about the cure.

This account lets us know that anyone filled with the fullness of the Holy Spirit can bring the healing presence of Jesus to any encounter. Peter clearly explains that it was not his power but the power of God that brought about this cure. Receiving God's personal love, the Holy Spirit, makes it possible for us to help people experience physical, emotional, and spiritual healing. This power

The Healing of the Crippled Man

remained a normal part of the Christian community for the first three centuries. It is present today to those who take time to prepare and receive the full infusion of the Holy Spirit and are open to the gifts of the Spirit.

The story goes on to say that the cured man went into the temple with Peter and John, "walking and jumping and praising God," and the people were filled with wonder and amazement. This phrase reminds me of the time we were in Malta teaching people how to prepare themselves and then pray with others for healing. On our last evening, we celebrated a healing Eucharist attended by at least 3000 people. After sharing Communion, we offered prayers for healing. Many reported pains going away, and one man rose from his wheelchair and walked around. Doctors who were present verified the healings. One of the priests celebrating with me asked us to pray for his sister, who could not be there because she had fallen, hurt her leg, and could not walk. We did pray for her. The next morning when we were at the airport getting ready to leave, a woman came to us walking and jumping and praising God. She was the sister of the priest. Right when we interceded for her during the healing service, she felt power go through her in her room. Her leg was healed at that moment. We praised God together at the airport. A scriptural response to healing is to praise God for the gift.

QUESTIONS FOR REFECTION/DISCUSSION

1. Have you ever experienced the healing power of Jesus in your life? Share.

2. How has your faith-relationship with Jesus brought life and healing to others?

3. Have you ever prayed with someone for healing? How did you bring the power of God's love, the Holy Spirit, to the encounter?

4. How did Peter bring this man beyond his human expectation for money to the divine expectation of healing? How can we invite people to expect the greater treasures of life?

5. How did this cure draw more people to be open to this new way of living the fullness of life? What could this do for our world today?

TIME OF PRAYER WITH EACH OTHER

PRACTICAL APPLICATION

Ask God to direct you regarding praying with someone for healing. If you feel the call, go and pray with them. Try to get them to feel God's personal love for them by your presence, your reading of God's word and your prayer. If they feel God's love, healing will happen on some level. Give God the praise.

Session 5

Self-Assurance with the Holy Spirit

PRAYER

READ ACTS 4:1-24

The priests and the captain of the temple guard and the Sadducees came up to Peter and John while they were speaking to the people. ²They were greatly disturbed because the apostles were teaching the people, proclaiming in Jesus the resurrection of the dead. ³They seized Peter and John and, because it was evening, they put them in jail until the next day. ⁴But many who heard the message believed; so the number of men who believed grew to about five thousand.

⁵The next day the rulers, the elders and the teachers of the law met in Jerusalem. ⁶Annas the high priest was there, and so were Caiaphas, John, Alexander, and others of the high priest's family. ⁷They had Peter and John brought before them and began to question them: "By what power or what name did you do this?"

⁸Then Peter, filled with the Holy Spirit, said to them: "Rulers and elders of the people! ⁹If we are being called to account today for an act of kindness shown to a man who was lame and are being asked how he was healed, ¹⁰then know this, you and all the people of Israel: It is by the name of Jesus Christ of Nazareth,

whom you crucified but whom God raised from the dead, that this man stands before you healed. ¹¹Jesus is

'the stone you builders rejected,
which has become the cornerstone.'

¹²Salvation is found in no one else, for there is no other name under heaven given to mankind by which we must be saved."

¹³When they saw the courage of Peter and John and realized that they were unschooled, ordinary men, they were astonished and they took note that these men had been with Jesus. ¹⁴But since they could see the man who had been healed standing there with them, there was nothing they could say. ¹⁵So they ordered them to withdraw from the Sanhedrin and then conferred together. ¹⁶"What are we going to do with these men?" they asked. "Everyone living in Jerusalem knows they have performed a notable sign, and we cannot deny it. ¹⁷But to stop this thing from spreading any further among the people, we must warn them to speak no longer to anyone in this name."

¹⁸Then they called them in again and commanded them not to speak or teach at all in the name of Jesus. ¹⁹But Peter and John replied, "Which is right in God's eyes: to listen to you, or to him? You be the judges! ²⁰As for us, we cannot help speaking about what we have seen and heard."

²¹After further threats they let them go. They could not decide how to punish them, because all the people were praising God for what had happened. ²²For the man who was miraculously healed was over forty years old.

²³On their release, Peter and John went back to their own people and reported all that the chief priests and the elders had said to them. ²⁴When they heard this, they raised their voices together in prayer to God. "Sovereign Lord," they said, "you made the heavens and the earth and the sea, and everything in them.

ACTS 4:29-31

²⁹"Now, Lord, consider their threats and enable your servants to speak your word with great boldness. ³⁰Stretch out your hand to

Self-Assurance with the Holy Spirit

heal and perform signs and wonders through the name of your holy servant Jesus."

³¹After they prayed, the place where they were meeting was shaken. And they were all filled with the Holy Spirit and spoke the word of God boldly.

REFLECTION

Living the new life and continuing the saving mission of Jesus meant persecution for the first disciples. Even when the religious leaders tried to stop him, the Holy Spirit's power that filled Peter enabled him to continue preaching. With divine courage, Peter testified to the power source behind the healing of the crippled man. The cured man and the extraordinary self-assurance of Peter and John left the leaders amazed and speechless. Peter and John testify that they now live a life directed by God's voice, not human voices. The leaders recognized these men as "having been with Jesus" (verse thirteen). Jesus' presence was still with them. Filled by the Holy Spirit, they proclaimed that they could not help speaking about what they had heard and seen. They were listening to the voice from above.

Recall when Peter first saw a miracle of Jesus as he caught a great number of fish. He said, "Leave me, Lord, for I am a sinful man" (Luke 5:8). At that time, he was filled with guilt and shame. Here we see how this shameful fisherman from Galilee now has the courage and the strong self-identity to stand up to the religious leaders in Jerusalem. Being with Jesus and opening himself to the Holy Spirit transformed him into a leader willing to risk his life for the Master. Jesus' love brought healing to Peter's inner child. Recall how John, on the way to Jerusalem, was only concerned about the reward, about sitting on Jesus' right hand in the kingdom (Mark 10:35–37). Here we see all of that self-centeredness gone. Here we see two men who were transformed by the power of God's love. That is a miracle. It is also possible for us. We can each experience inner healing and become who God has created us to be.

Healing Miracles in Acts of the Apostles

The final verses of this section tell us about the miracle of a praying community. Peter and John did not stand alone before the leaders. They had a praying community behind them. This unified intercession has amazing power. The community also prayed for cures, signs and wonders that gave credence to their preaching.

The final verse tells of a "second Pentecost" with another filling of the Holy Spirit. It shook the building. Jesus was alive in his disciples, and his continuous outpouring of love empowered them for his divine mission. It is evident that there were a number of outpourings of the Holy Spirit.

One evening when we had prepared a group of people for a fresh anointing of the Holy Spirit, we invited each to come forward, if they chose, and receive prayer for this anointing. One young woman said earlier that she did not want that prayer. She was afraid. I understood. However, while we were praying with other people that evening, the floor in the church started to shake. She felt it, got up immediately and came up for prayer. She said afterward, "I was not going to miss that." The Holy Spirit is present in our world, inviting people to receive more love, more power, and more peace.

QUESTIONS FOR REFLECTION/DISCUSSION

1. What had to heal in Peter to arrive at this level of self-assurance (Luke 5:1–11, Mark 8:31–31, Matthew 26:69–75)?

2. How might we grow in the kind of courage and self-assurance we see in this scripture?

3. How has knowing Jesus shaped your character so that people might notice that you have "been with Jesus?" (verse 4:13)

Self-Assurance with the Holy Spirit

4. How might you find or create a community (if you do not have one) to pray for you when you need courage or empowerment for a specific mission?

5. Do you or your community need a "second Pentecost"? How might you help set the stage for that to happen?

6. What insight about living the Christian life did you receive from this session?

TIME OF PRAYER WITH EACH OTHER

PRACTICAL APPLICATION

Ask God to show you where you might be called to speak about Jesus with boldness. Go and do it.

Session 6

Many People Were Cured

PRAYER

READ ACTS 5:12–16

¹²The apostles performed many signs and wonders among the people. And all the believers used to meet together in Solomon's Colonnade. ¹³No one else dared join them, even though they were highly regarded by the people. ¹⁴Nevertheless, more and more men and women believed in the Lord and were added to their number. ¹⁵As a result, people brought the sick into the streets and laid them on beds and mats so that at least Peter's shadow might fall on some of them as he passed by. ¹⁶Crowds gathered also from the towns around Jerusalem, bringing their sick and those tormented by impure spirits, and all of them were healed.

REFLECTION

It is amazing to witness the power of God healing and setting people free. Acts of the Apostles is filled with demonstrations of energy that flows from being filled with the Holy Spirit. These verses describe the signs and wonders and the healings that happened as the early Christians continued Jesus' mission to bring the power of heaven to earth. The apostles were demonstrating the same power of God's love as Jesus did, and people were coming from all around to lay the sick at their feet. Peter must have radiated the presence of Jesus' love so strongly that people experienced healing when they got within the distance of his shadow. As healing communities and prayer ministers, we seek to create environments where people can feel surrounded by the safety and warmth of God's personal love for them. Our prayer gatherings, worship services, and sharing in Holy Communion are meant to create the setting for healing to happen.

As in the gospels, the healings drew people into a faith relationship with Jesus. This story says many more people became believers. The cures showed God's deep love for people, and if individuals returned that love and committed their life to God, they were made whole. Records show that these healings were a normal part of the Christian life for the first 300 years. Once the church stopped the baptism of the Holy Spirit and the outpouring of the gifts of the Spirit, healings were no longer normal but only seen among a few people who were open to this great power. As time went on, people created various explanations why healings were no longer normal in the church. In the last century, people started to experience this outpouring of the Holy Spirit again and witnessed healings happen through their prayers. Groups organized to learn more about Jesus' healing power and how to share it with others. This is how the Order of St. Luke (OSL) started. It continues to carry out this ministry today.

I remember coming to one small church that was declining in membership and on the verge of closing. I suggested doing an area-wide healing service on New Year's Eve, five weeks after I arrived. Some leaders were hesitant about this idea, but they all showed up for this new event. The small church held sixty-five people in the pews, so I asked that we get at least fifty extra chairs. On the evening of the healing service, 125 people packed the church. There was a tremendous outpouring of God's love that evening. One woman came with such crippled-up hands that she could hardly hold anything. She even had a disability license plate for her car. She and her husband were so overwhelmed with their experience of God's love during the service that they left the church shaking. A couple of weeks later, she came to my office and handed me her disability license plate and said, "I won't be needing this anymore. My hands have healed since the night of the healing service." She learned to play guitar after her healing and became one of our great music ministers. She and her husband became leaders in our church.

Many others wanted to learn more about the power of the Holy Spirit after that service, so I offered the *Spiritual Enrichment Seminars* and scripture studies. The church grew to five times its original size and became a healing center for people all around. Many people became believers and were empowered by the Holy Spirit. Some people would walk into the church and tears would flow from their eyes. They were overwhelmed at the feeling of God's love in that place.

QUESTIONS FOR REFLECTION/DISCUSSION

1. What do you think it felt like to be laying on a cot sick and then experience healing?

2. What do you imagine it would have been like to be in the crowd when the power of God's love was manifest in cures?

3. What could you do to help your Christian community be open to the healing power of God?

4. Do you know people who came to faith in Jesus because they felt the healing and transforming power of God's love? Share the story.

5. What would it be like if divine healings were normal in the churches today as they were for the first three centuries? Would you want to be part of such a church?

TIME OF PRAYER WITH EACH OTHER

PRACTICAL APPLICATION

Pray about whether Jesus is calling you to learn more about his healing ministry. If you feel the call, seek resources to begin the journey. You might check out the website for the Order of St. Luke, *www.OSLToday.org.*

SESSION 7

The Anointing of Deacons

PRAYER

READ ACTS 6:1-7

In those days when the number of disciples was increasing, the Hellenistic Jews among them complained against the Hebraic Jews because their widows were being overlooked in the daily distribution of food. ²So the Twelve gathered all the disciples together and said, "It would not be right for us to neglect the ministry of the word of God in order to wait on tables. ³Brothers and sisters, choose seven men from among you who are known to be full of the Spirit and wisdom. We will turn this responsibility over to them ⁴and will give our attention to prayer and the ministry of the word."

⁵This proposal pleased the whole group. They chose Stephen, a man full of faith and of the Holy Spirit; also Philip, Procorus, Nicanor, Timon, Parmenas, and Nicolas from Antioch, a convert to Judaism. ⁶They presented these men to the apostles, who prayed and laid their hands on them.

The Anointing of Deacons

⁷So the word of God spread. The number of disciples in Jerusalem increased rapidly, and a large number of priests became obedient to the faith.

REFLECTION

The Christian community had its growing pains. As more people joined them, they needed more ministers. In this account, we read how there was inequality in the distribution of food. The apostles had to raise up more leaders so that they could continue their work of "prayer and ministry of the word." It is significant that the apostles kept doing what they were anointed to do. God needs the surrendered gifts of many people to change the world. There are many things to do in a Christian community. One role of leaders is to recognize who are anointed by the Holy Spirit for particular ministries and then encourage and empower these people to carry them out. The apostles called upon people who were "known to be full of the Spirit and wisdom" or another translation, "deeply spiritual and prudent" (verse three) to serve those in need.

The anointing of deacons was to gather money and resources and then distribute them fairly to those in need. They would collect money and goods for the poor and then allocate these gifts as God directed. Since human beings by nature are somewhat selfish, deacons have to stay focused on God's purpose for the resources they oversee. They cannot be self-centered. Their interior spirituality and attentive listening to God are crucial for their ministry.

One time when I pastored a community, someone asked me why I did not have deacons. They did not see any deacons helping me in the liturgical service on Sunday. I said, "I have three deacons. One runs the food pantry, one runs the thrift store and one oversees the church finances." They did not dress like deacons, nor were they "ordained" like some deacons, but they were empowered to do the anointed deacon work in that community. They allowed me to concentrate on prayer and ministry of the word. Their ministry was vital in that church for God's mission to be carried out.

Healing Miracles in Acts of the Apostles

This account tells us that the early Christian community had to keep listening and adjusting to new growth and changes. Walking in the power of the Holy Spirit involves daily listening and re-energizing. The miracles are not found just in healings but in Spirit-led service. Giving food or clothes in Jesus' name, like cures, is an invitation for people to become believers. When those gifts are accompanied by the witness of Jesus' love and an invitation to draw close to him, then the gospel message spreads. That is a miracle.

QUESTIONS FOR REFLECTION/DISCUSSION

1. What can we learn, in this passage, from the response of the apostles about ministry and church growth?

2. What special anointing do you have for your ministry in the Christian community? How are you currently using that gift?

3. The apostles laid hands on the chosen men to set them apart as deacons. What various meanings does the laying on of hands have in your Christian community?

4. In your daily prayer and listening, do you feel guidance and empowerment for your ministry? Explain.

The Anointing of Deacons

5. How do you discern God's anointing on someone? How do you affirm them in that anointing?

6. What insight about living the Christian life did you receive from this session?

TIME OF PRAYER WITH EACH OTHER

PRACTICAL APPLICATION

Take time to pray and watch people in your community. If you feel called, let them know that you see a gift in them for Jesus' mission.

Session 8

The Miracle of Stephen

PRAYER

READ ACTS 6:8–15

⁸Now Stephen, a man full of God's grace and power, performed great wonders and signs among the people. ⁹Opposition arose, however, from members of the Synagogue of the Freedmen (as it was called)—Jews of Cyrene and Alexandria as well as the provinces of Cilicia and Asia—who began to argue with Stephen. ¹⁰But they could not stand up against the wisdom the Spirit gave him as he spoke.

¹¹Then they secretly persuaded some men to say, "We have heard Stephen speak blasphemous words against Moses and against God."

¹²So they stirred up the people and the elders and the teachers of the law. They seized Stephen and brought him before the Sanhedrin. ¹³They produced false witnesses, who testified, "This fellow never stops speaking against this holy place and against the law. ¹⁴For we have heard him say that this Jesus of Nazareth will destroy this place and change the customs Moses handed down to us."

The Miracle of Stephen

¹⁵All who were sitting in the Sanhedrin looked intently at Stephen, and they saw that his face was like the face of an angel.

ACTS 7:54-60

⁵⁴When the members of the Sanhedrin heard this, they were furious and gnashed their teeth at him. ⁵⁵But Stephen, full of the Holy Spirit, looked up to heaven and saw the glory of God, and Jesus standing at the right hand of God. ⁵⁶"Look," he said, "I see heaven open and the Son of Man standing at the right hand of God."

⁵⁷At this they covered their ears and, yelling at the top of their voices, they all rushed at him, ⁵⁸dragged him out of the city and began to stone him. Meanwhile, the witnesses laid their coats at the feet of a young man named Saul.

⁵⁹While they were stoning him, Stephen prayed, "Lord Jesus, receive my spirit." ⁶⁰Then he fell on his knees and cried out, "Lord, do not hold this sin against them." When he had said this, he fell asleep.

And Saul approved of their killing him.

REFLECTION

The anointing of the Holy Spirit comes in many forms. In this session, we see how the religious leaders were no match for Stephen's "wisdom or the Spirit by whom he spoke" (verse ten). We do not always know what to say in certain circumstances, but the Spirit gives us words if we are open and listening. Jesus had promised this gift to his followers. Living in the power of the Holy Spirit gives us wisdom greater than that of the world.

There was a priest in our church when I was in grade school. He never made deep theological statements, but he could tell simple stories that helped me understand Jesus. He had a wisdom that was inspiring, and that wisdom inspired me to be a priest. I also met a priest in college seminary who invited me to a retreat on the Holy Spirit. I resisted coming to the retreat, telling him that

I knew the Holy Spirit. He did not force the issue but, in his wisdom, suggested that I was welcome to try it. I came to the retreat, and through his teaching, I discovered the baptism of the Holy Spirit and began to see the gifts of the Spirit operate in my life. His wisdom richly blessed me and many others. That retreat opened me to the healing power of Jesus in my life and in the world today.

Stephen not only demonstrated great wisdom but also gave witness to the deep, inner peace that flows from a life in the Spirit. The story says that Stephen's face "was like the face of an angel" and that he looked up "and saw the glory of God." He was willing to accept death for his God because he was getting his direction from above. He was empowered by his vision of God.

His ability to forgive those who were stoning him was a God-directed act. He modeled Jesus on the cross. He knew that the ultimate way to healing was to forgive those who hurt him. This gesture was a miracle, empowered by the Holy Spirit. His witness encourages us to forgive and to stand fast in the face of ridicule or persecution. This story reminds us that speaking Jesus' message in the world may involve suffering, ridicule, and even physical pain, but such pain is made holy by our faithfulness to the Master's voice.

Then the final miracle occurs. Stephen's acceptance of death for Jesus with forgiveness in his heart was witnessed by Saul (Paul). I believe that Paul's witnessing of the way Stephen died was the beginning of his conversion and ultimate life lived in the power of the Holy Spirit. This passage tells us that one of the "deeply spiritual and prudent" deacons demonstrated another way of "feeding" those in need.

QUESTIONS FOR REFLECTION/DISCUSSION

1. What do you think gave Stephen the courage to die for his faith? What did he see that others did not see?

2. Have you ever received a word of wisdom when you did not know what to say? Share.

3. What things do you think Stephen did to make him ready for this day?

4. How have you experienced forgiveness opening the door to healing?

5. Have you ever had "stones" thrown at you, and you did not retaliate? What does that do to the person throwing them?

6. What insight about living the Christian life did you receive from this session?

TIME OF PRAYER WITH EACH OTHER

PRACTICAL APPLICATION

Pray about whom you might need to forgive. Take a step toward forgiving them.

SESSION 9

Miracles in Samaria

PRAYER

READ ACTS 8:1–25

On that day a great persecution broke out against the church in Jerusalem, and all except the apostles were scattered throughout Judea and Samaria. ²Godly men buried Stephen and mourned deeply for him. ³But Saul began to destroy the church. Going from house to house, he dragged off both men and women and put them in prison.

⁴Those who had been scattered preached the word wherever they went. ⁵Philip went down to a city in Samaria and proclaimed the Messiah there. ⁶When the crowds heard Philip and saw the signs he performed, they all paid close attention to what he said. ⁷For with shrieks, impure spirits came out of many, and many who were paralyzed or lame were healed. ⁸So there was great joy in that city.

⁹Now for some time a man named Simon had practiced sorcery in the city and amazed all the people of Samaria. He boasted that he was someone great, ¹⁰and all the people, both high and low, gave him their attention and exclaimed, "This man is rightly called

Miracles in Samaria

the Great Power of God." [11]They followed him because he had amazed them for a long time with his sorcery. [12]But when they believed Philip as he proclaimed the good news of the kingdom of God and the name of Jesus Christ, they were baptized, both men and women. [13]Simon himself believed and was baptized. And he followed Philip everywhere, astonished by the great signs and miracles he saw.

[14]When the apostles in Jerusalem heard that Samaria had accepted the word of God, they sent Peter and John to Samaria. [15]When they arrived, they prayed for the new believers there that they might receive the Holy Spirit, [16]because the Holy Spirit had not yet come on any of them; they had simply been baptized in the name of the Lord Jesus. [17]Then Peter and John placed their hands on them, and they received the Holy Spirit.

[18]When Simon saw that the Spirit was given at the laying on of the apostles' hands, he offered them money [19]and said, "Give me also this ability so that everyone on whom I lay my hands may receive the Holy Spirit."

[20]Peter answered: "May your money perish with you, because you thought you could buy the gift of God with money! [21]You have no part or share in this ministry, because your heart is not right before God. [22]Repent of this wickedness and pray to the Lord in the hope that he may forgive you for having such a thought in your heart. [23]For I see that you are full of bitterness and captive to sin."

[24]Then Simon answered, "Pray to the Lord for me so that nothing you have said may happen to me."

[25]After they had further proclaimed the word of the Lord and testified about Jesus, Peter and John returned to Jerusalem, preaching the gospel in many Samaritan villages.

REFLECTION

In this account, we see the movement of the Holy Spirit, even when worldly power tried to stop it. God can make holy even unholy situations. The persecution of Christians in Jerusalem led to the spreading of Christianity to many other countries. It set the stage for Philip to go to Samaria to preach Jesus' message. As he ministered, unclean spirits came out of people, and many paralyzed and crippled people were cured. The miracles continued. As we have seen before, the healing and deliverance that Philip did gave credence to the message he spoke. He was doing the mission of Jesus. It says that there was "great joy" in that place, and joy is one of the fruits of the Holy Spirit.

We also read about Peter and John coming to Samaria to pray for a second anointing for the people. They were believers but they needed this second anointing to experience the fullness of the Holy Spirit. After the resurrection, the apostles were believers too, but they also needed an occasion to receive the full power of the Holy Spirit. This happened to them at Pentecost. By the end of the third century, the church stopped praying for this second anointing, this infusion of the Holy Spirit, and that is when Christians no longer experienced healing as the norm.

I have come into communities of faith who had not received this outpouring of the Holy Spirit. They were believers but they were not empowered. I developed that six-week retreat series, the *Spiritual Enrichment Seminars*, to invite people to experience that outpouring. It helps them feel God's personal love for them, intentionally surrender their life to Jesus, take a moral inventory and confess if needed, and then pray for a full outpouring of the Holy Spirit. This retreat has brought many people to experience the overwhelming love of God, to receive the gifts of the Holy Spirit, have a desire to read Scripture, participate more fully in the mission of Jesus, and to pray with others for healing. Miracles started to happen in those communities. If Christians are going to do what Jesus has commissioned us to do, I believe we have to receive this second anointing, this infusion of the Holy Spirit. Churches might consider creating an occasion for adult members to prepare for and receive the full anointing of God's personal love, the Holy Spirit. If people knew it was available, they might seek it and request it.

Miracles in Samaria

In this story we read that Simon could not receive the anointing of the Holy Spirit because his heart "was not right before God." Many people who seek this out pouring of the Holy Spirit realize that they need to take a moral inventory and then confess past failures. Repenting opens the way for Jesus to enter their life in a deeper and fuller way. The experience of Jesus' extravagant mercy allows us to feel his love in a deeper way and to live in the power of that love every day.

QUESTIONS FOR REFLECTION/DISCUSSION

1. The persecution of the Christians in Jerusalem led to the spread of Christianity to other countries. How has God helped you see good in what appears to be a destructive situation?

2. Philip went around preaching, healing, and dispelling unclean spirits. What do you think he did to prepare for this ministry?

3. We read that Simon held people under the spell of his magic. What things hold people "under a spell" today? How can we help set them free?

4. Philip reached out to Samaritans who were outcasts to Jews. How has the power of the Holy Spirit helped you reach out to "outcasts" in your life?

Healing Miracles in Acts of the Apostles

5. Peter and John brought an anointing of the Holy Spirit to believers in Samaria. How could you participate in bringing such an anointing to people you know?

TIME OF PRAYER WITH EACH OTHER

PRACTICAL APPLICATION

Peter and John brought the good news of healing and the Holy Spirit to people they met on their way home. Tell someone of a healing that you have seen or experienced.

SESSION 10

The Miraculous Encounter

PRAYER

READ ACTS 9:1–30

Meanwhile, Saul was still breathing out murderous threats against the Lord's disciples. He went to the high priest ²and asked him for letters to the synagogues in Damascus, so that if he found any there who belonged to the Way, whether men or women, he might take them as prisoners to Jerusalem. ³As he neared Damascus on his journey, suddenly a light from heaven flashed around him. ⁴He fell to the ground and heard a voice say to him, "Saul, Saul, why do you persecute me?"

⁵"Who are you, Lord?" Saul asked.

"I am Jesus, whom you are persecuting," he replied. ⁶"Now get up and go into the city, and you will be told what you must do."

⁷The men traveling with Saul stood there speechless; they heard the sound but did not see anyone. ⁸Saul got up from the ground, but when he opened his eyes he could see nothing. So they led him by the hand into Damascus. ⁹For three days he was blind, and did not eat or drink anything.

Healing Miracles in Acts of the Apostles

¹⁰In Damascus there was a disciple named Ananias. The Lord called to him in a vision, "Ananias!"

"Yes, Lord," he answered.

¹¹The Lord told him, "Go to the house of Judas on Straight Street and ask for a man from Tarsus named Saul, for he is praying. ¹²In a vision he has seen a man named Ananias come and place his hands on him to restore his sight."

¹³"Lord," Ananias answered, "I have heard many reports about this man and all the harm he has done to your holy people in Jerusalem. ¹⁴And he has come here with authority from the chief priests to arrest all who call on your name."

¹⁵But the Lord said to Ananias, "Go! This man is my chosen instrument to proclaim my name to the Gentiles and their kings and to the people of Israel. ¹⁶I will show him how much he must suffer for my name."

¹⁷Then Ananias went to the house and entered it. Placing his hands on Saul, he said, "Brother Saul, the Lord—Jesus, who appeared to you on the road as you were coming here—has sent me so that you may see again and be filled with the Holy Spirit." ¹⁸Immediately, something like scales fell from Saul's eyes, and he could see again. He got up and was baptized, ¹⁹and after taking some food, he regained his strength.

Saul spent several days with the disciples in Damascus. ²⁰At once he began to preach in the synagogues that Jesus is the Son of God. ²¹All those who heard him were astonished and asked, "Isn't he the man who raised havoc in Jerusalem among those who call on this name? And hasn't he come here to take them as prisoners to the chief priests?" ²²Yet Saul grew more and more powerful and baffled the Jews living in Damascus by proving that Jesus is the Messiah.

²³After many days had gone by, there was a conspiracy among the Jews to kill him, ²⁴but Saul learned of their plan. Day and night they kept close watch on the city gates in order to kill him. ²⁵But his followers took him by night and lowered him in a basket through an opening in the wall.

²⁶When he came to Jerusalem, he tried to join the disciples, but they were all afraid of him, not believing that he really was

The Miraculous Encounter

a disciple. ²⁷But Barnabas took him and brought him to the apostles. He told them how Saul on his journey had seen the Lord and that the Lord had spoken to him, and how in Damascus he had preached fearlessly in the name of Jesus. ²⁸So Saul stayed with them and moved about freely in Jerusalem, speaking boldly in the name of the Lord. ²⁹He talked and debated with the Hellenistic Jews, but they tried to kill him. ³⁰When the believers learned of this, they took him down to Caesarea and sent him off to Tarsus.

REFLECTION

The conversion of Paul was an unprecedented miracle. There is no way this man so set on destroying Christians would make an about-face on the road to Damascus except that the risen Jesus intervened. Paul went from one world to another world, from being blind to seeing. Jesus said that from now on, he would be told what to do. Paul was now directed by a new voice, a voice that would lead numerous people to wholeness and salvation. He was the "instrument Jesus had chosen" to bring the message of salvation to the Gentiles. With his background and education, he was able to speak to Jews and Gentiles alike. Because of Paul's submission to this calling, we Gentiles, are privileged to know about Jesus. God chooses us also with our gifts, augmented by the gifts of the Holy Spirit, to proclaim his message to the world in words and actions. God needs only our "yes."

Many people participated in the transformation of Paul's life. His conversion was completed by the obedience of a man named Ananias. Ananias had to step through his fear and prejudice to go and empower Paul with the prayer for the Holy Spirit. Ananias resists Jesus' request at first thinking, "Is not this the man who has been persecuting Christians?" Jesus pretty much says, "No, this is not the same man. He is a new man. He may look like the same man, but he is different. This is the man I have chosen to take my message to the Gentiles." God's anointing on Paul made him a different man, and God's plan for him was beyond rational thought. Ananias finally went as requested. His "yes" was crucial in getting

Paul equipped for his awesome ministry. We also read how Paul's disciples kept him from getting killed in Damascus. They all risked their lives as they participated in God's work of transforming this persecutor of the Christians to a powerful, Spirit-led apostle.

Toward the end of this story, we hear of another man, Barnabas, who was the bridge that connected Paul to the apostles in Jerusalem. He played a significant role in connecting Paul to the leaders of the church. That connection would be very significant in the growth and ministry of the early church.

The role of introducing people to others is very important for the community's growth and the enrichment of its members. In my first parish, a doctor came to speak on healing. He shared how prayer for healing, combined with his medical practice, brought about greater healings than he could do himself. I asked him more about his ministry and he introduced me to ACTHeals, a national organization of professionals filled with the Holy Spirit, who pray with their patients for healing. I joined that group, and it expanded my ministry and allowed me further connections that greatly enriched my life and the lives of many others. I am very grateful to that doctor.

Paul's teachings and letters expanded Jesus' message into practical applications for Jews and Gentiles alike. His writings have guided the Christian community throughout history. Paul's letters show us a man totally committed to Jesus and one who would do anything to honor his Master. He let go of his old world so that he might be totally filled with Jesus. He wrote, "For Jesus' sake I have accepted the loss of all thing, and I consider them so much rubbish, that I may gain Christ and be found in him" (Phil 3:8). The conversion of Paul was a very significant miracle for the entire church.

QUESTIONS FOR REFLECTION/DISCUSSION

1. How has an encounter with Jesus changed your plans along life's journey?

The Miraculous Encounter

2. How has God used you to help someone else know Jesus?

3. In what way might you need to get past your fear or prejudice to proclaim the message of Jesus?

4. Barnabas introduced Paul to the apostles. When have you introduced a person or teaching to church leaders as a means of proclaiming the gospel?

5. How have the letters of Paul opened your mind and heart to the presence and power of the Holy Spirit?

6. What insight about living the Christian life did you receive from this session?

TIME OF PRAYER WITH EACH OTHER

PRACTICAL APPLICATION

Read Paul's letter to the Philippians. Let it influence how you live life.

SESSION 11

Miracles in Lydda and Joppa

PRAYER

READ ACTS 9:31–43

³¹Then the church throughout Judea, Galilee, and Samaria enjoyed a time of peace and was strengthened. Living in the fear of the Lord and encouraged by the Holy Spirit, it increased in numbers.

³²As Peter traveled about the country, he went to visit the Lord's people who lived in Lydda. ³³There he found a man named Aeneas, who was paralyzed and had been bedridden for eight years. ³⁴"Aeneas," Peter said to him, "Jesus Christ heals you. Get up and roll up your mat." Immediately Aeneas got up. ³⁵All those who lived in Lydda and Sharon saw him and turned to the Lord.

³⁶In Joppa there was a disciple named Tabitha (in Greek her name is Dorcas); she was always doing good and helping the poor. ³⁷About that time she became sick and died, and her body was washed and placed in an upstairs room. ³⁸Lydda was near Joppa; so when the disciples heard that Peter was in Lydda, they sent two men to him and urged him, "Please come at once!"

³⁹Peter went with them, and when he arrived he was taken upstairs to the room. All the widows stood around him, crying and

Miracles in Lydda and Joppa

showing him the robes and other clothing that Dorcas had made while she was still with them.

⁴⁰Peter sent them all out of the room; then he got down on his knees and prayed. Turning toward the dead woman, he said, "Tabitha, get up." She opened her eyes, and seeing Peter she sat up. ⁴¹He took her by the hand and helped her to her feet. Then he called for the believers, especially the widows, and presented her to them alive. ⁴²This became known all over Joppa, and many people believed in the Lord. ⁴³Peter stayed in Joppa for some time with a tanner named Simon.

REFLECTION

This scripture section reminds us of how important the Holy Spirit was and is for the vibrancy of the Christian community. It was being built up and making steady progress. The stories continue to affirm that progress as they describe healings and miracles. We read how Peter arrived in Lydda and cured a paralytic in the name of Jesus. He gave a simple word of command. This was not his word but it was a word from Jesus. He expected Jesus' power to be accessible to him and proclaimed it with confidence. His daily listening for the Master's voice allowed him to know when Jesus was going to move in power. Being connected to that power, that transforming love, that divine energy, is the core of the Christian healing ministry. The result was that the man was cured, and all the inhabitants of that area became believers. That was the ultimate goal. That is what Jesus had modeled. He wanted people to be in a saving, faith-relationship with him.

Two men from Joppa came to Lydda asking Peter if he might please come without delay to their town because a generous, gifted woman had died. Peter came to Joppa and went to the room where the body was. Peter sent out all the people. He knelt and prayed. His prayer led him to give this word of command, "Tabitha, rise up." Because it was a word from Jesus, one Peter received in prayer, it had the same effect as Jesus' words (See Luke 8:54). Living a life in the Spirit involves continual listening for direction and receiving empowerment. Again, many became believers because of this miracle. The early Christian community changed the way people thought and lived by demonstrating God's healing power through their ministry. The world was impoverished when the Christian church stopped doing that as a normal part of preaching the gospel. We must begin again.

The miracle of raising the dead still happens at times in our world today. Several years ago, I received a testimony about a youth group who witnessed the raising of a stillborn baby. They were evangelizing in Guatemala. They came to one woman's house and asked if they could pray with her for anything. She said she just had a stillborn baby the day before. They prayed with the woman that she would find comfort. One of the girls in the group, Julia, said a number of times, "We really need to pray over the baby's body," which was in the back room. She asked the mother if she could go and pray for the baby. Julia picked up the baby, who had been dead outside the womb for twenty-seven hours. The group prayed over the body for thirty to forty minutes. At one point, Julia screamed out to God that she believed this baby could be raised from the dead. Within a few minutes, the baby started to move. Then it began to cry. The mother came rushing in, overjoyed to see her baby alive. The whole village heard of it and came by. The group of young people explained the message of Jesus to the ninty villagers gathered, and they all received Jesus. Five days later, the group returned to the village, and the baby was doing well.

There are other stories like this as well. Doctor Chauncey Crandall, a well-known cardiologist, tells the story in his book, *Raising the Dead*, of his experience of seeing a dead man come back to life. The man had a massive heart attack, and after forty minutes and many shock attempts in the emergency room to revive him, he was pronounced dead. After the staff left the room, only one nurse was there preparing the body for the family to see it. Doctor Chauncey finished his report and was on his way to his office when he felt the call to go back and pray for the man to be raised from the dead. As he prayed, the ER doctor walked into the room, and Chauncey asked him to shock the man one more

Miracles in Lydda and Joppa

time. It took some serious convincing, but finally, he consented. After that shock, the man came alive and he immediately had a perfect heartbeat. The nurse in the room screamed. She did not know what to do. They took the man to ICU. A couple days later, he was sitting up in bed doing fine.

It is hard to understand the ways of God and these miraculous events. What is clear is that the power of the risen Jesus is accessible on earth. These stories challenge us to draw close to him and continually listen for his direction, and, when called, to step out and pray as he guides us. Being a channel of Jesus' healing and saving power is an awesome and exciting mission. It is what Jesus has commissioned us to do. We begin with receiving his empowerment and then seeing where he directs.

QUESTIONS FOR REFLECTION/DISCUSSION

1. How is your Christian community "being built up and making steady progress?"

2. How do you think Peter was able to bring the living Presence of Jesus to these encounters?

3. How is our prayer of intercession like the two men who requested Peter to come? How significant is this ministry of intercession as we seek to offer healing in Jesus' name?

4. Why do you think Peter made all the people go out of the room before he prayed and gave a word of command?

5. What would you do if you saw someone raised from the dead? Why do you think Peter stayed on in Joppa?

6. What do you think Tabitha did after she was raised? How do you think she lived?

TIME OF PRAYER WITH EACH OTHER

PRACTICAL APPLICATION

Write out your Rule of Life; that is, the things you do to stay immersed in the power of the Holy Spirit.

SESSION 12

The Miracle of Cornelius

PRAYER

READ ACTS 10:1-8

At Caesarea there was a man named Cornelius, a centurion in what was known as the Italian Regiment. ²He and all his family were devout and God-fearing; he gave generously to those in need and prayed to God regularly. ³One day at about three in the afternoon he had a vision. He distinctly saw an angel of God, who came to him and said, "Cornelius!"

⁴Cornelius stared at him in fear. "What is it, Lord?" he asked.

The angel answered, "Your prayers and gifts to the poor have come up as a memorial offering before God. ⁵Now send men to Joppa to bring back a man named Simon who is called Peter. ⁶He is staying with Simon the tanner, whose house is by the sea."

⁷When the angel who spoke to him had gone, Cornelius called two of his servants and a devout soldier who was one of his attendants. ⁸He told them everything that had happened and sent them to Joppa.

Healing Miracles in Acts of the Apostles

ACTS 10:17-28

17 While Peter was wondering about the meaning of the vision, the men sent by Cornelius found out where Simon's house was and stopped at the gate. 18 They called out, asking if Simon who was known as Peter was staying there.

19 While Peter was still thinking about the vision, the Spirit said to him, "Simon, two men are looking for you. 20 So get up and go downstairs. Do not hesitate to go with them, for I have sent them."

21 Peter went down and said to the men, "I'm the one you're looking for. Why have you come?"

22 The men replied, "We have come from Cornelius the centurion. He is a righteous and God-fearing man, who is respected by all the Jewish people. A holy angel told him to ask you to come to his house so that he could hear what you have to say." 23 Then Peter invited the men into the house to be his guests.

The next day Peter started out with them, and some of the believers from Joppa went along. 24 The following day he arrived in Caesarea. Cornelius was expecting them and had called together his relatives and close friends. 25 As Peter entered the house, Cornelius met him and fell at his feet in reverence. 26 But Peter made him get up. "Stand up," he said, "I am only a man myself."

27 While talking with him, Peter went inside and found a large gathering of people. 28 He said to them: "You are well aware that it is against our law for a Jew to associate with or visit a Gentile. But God has shown me that I should not call anyone impure or unclean.

ACTS 10:34-36

34 Then Peter began to speak: "I now realize how true it is that God does not show favoritism 35 but accepts from every nation the one who fears him and does what is right. 36 You know the message God sent to the people of Israel, announcing the good news of peace through Jesus Christ, who is Lord of all.

The Miracle of Cornelius

ACTS 10:44-48

⁴⁴While Peter was still speaking these words, the Holy Spirit came on all who heard the message. ⁴⁵The circumcised believers who had come with Peter were astonished that the gift of the Holy Spirit had been poured out even on Gentiles. ⁴⁶For they heard them speaking in tongues and praising God.

Then Peter said, ⁴⁷"Surely no one can stand in the way of their being baptized with water. They have received the Holy Spirit just as we have." ⁴⁸So he ordered that they be baptized in the name of Jesus Christ. Then they asked Peter to stay with them for a few days.

REFLECTION

This account offers us the amazing story of how the early Christians were directed to invite non-Jews into the Christian community. It was the miracle that happened in Cornelius' house that broke through the limits of their religious practice and opened the door for Gentiles to become Christians. It was a monumental change for the early church, and it happened because Peter and others were listening to and obedient to the Holy Spirit. Peter first had a vision indicating that all food was clean, which took him beyond his Jewish beliefs. This vision would start to open the door for him to be with Gentiles. Soon after the vision, he received a message to go with the two men asking for him. They were requesting him to come to a Gentile's house in Caesarea. This was no small request. They asked Peter to enter a Gentile's home, which was "unlawful" for a Jew to do. The Spirit, however, had told Peter to go with them without hesitation. It was a miracle that Peter went. He had to let Jesus heal all his prejudices and false assumptions concerning Gentiles. He had to risk his relationships with his Jewish friends and step where he had never gone before. God had made it clear that Peter was to break from his old ways and walk in the power of the Holy Spirit. He realized that God "accepts from every nation the one who fears him and does what is right." Right behavior or holy living is the only criteria for God's acceptance. Peter's obedience to the Master's voice sets the stage for the second miracle.

When Peter arrived at Cornelius' house, a whole group was waiting for him to speak. God was orchestrating a breakthrough moment. The crowd was ready to hear "everything the Lord has commanded you to tell us" (verse thirty-three). God revealed that his Son, Jesus, was inviting all people into a saving relationship through faith. As Peter spoke to Cornelius and his household, God sent the Holy Spirit to fall on them, and they began to speak in tongues and glorify God. It was a miracle. It surprised the Jews who were with Peter, and it broke open a whole new realm of ministry. God was in charge, and the early Christians would be stretched beyond where they ever thought they would go. Jesus came to save all people, and these first Jewish Christians would have to minister "outside the box" and enter the Gentile territory with the message and power of Jesus. Their journey would have to be directed by the Holy Spirit because there was no road map for this unchartered territory. Because they accepted the guidance of the Holy Spirit, the message of Jesus has come to us.

We all meet people of different nationalities and religious backgrounds. Jesus' commission calls us to invite all of them into a relationship with him. As we saw in session three, all who *metanoia*, all who are willing to turn around and walk in the way of Jesus, can share in the fullness of life that he offers.

QUESTIONS FOR REFLECTION/DISCUSSION

1. How has God called you to broaden your vision of people and his plan for you?

2. How might we change our language and old religious practices to proclaim the gospel effectively to more people?

The Miracle of Cornelius

3. What things in Christian practice can we change, and what must we not change to remain faithful to Jesus?

4. Can you describe a time when you knew you had to do something outside the box for God?

5. After Peter saw the Spirit fall on Cornelius and his household, he realized he could not interfere with God's movement. How have you gotten out of the way when God was moving in your life?

TIME OF PRAYER WITH EACH OTHER

PRACTICAL APPLICATION

Ask God to show you to whom you might speak about God's love and forgiveness.

Session 13

Miracles in Antioch

PRAYER

READ ACTS 11:19-30

¹⁹Now those who had been scattered by the persecution that broke out when Stephen was killed traveled as far as Phoenicia, Cyprus, and Antioch, spreading the word only among Jews. ²⁰Some of them, however, men from Cyprus and Cyrene, went to Antioch and began to speak to Greeks also, telling them the good news about the Lord Jesus. ²¹The Lord's hand was with them, and a great number of people believed and turned to the Lord.

²²News of this reached the church in Jerusalem, and they sent Barnabas to Antioch. ²³When he arrived and saw what the grace of God had done, he was glad and encouraged them all to remain true to the Lord with all their hearts. ²⁴He was a good man, full of the Holy Spirit and faith, and a great number of people were brought to the Lord.

²⁵Then Barnabas went to Tarsus to look for Saul, ²⁶and when he found him, he brought him to Antioch. So for a whole year Barnabas and Saul met with the church and taught great numbers of people. The disciples were called Christians first at Antioch.

Miracles in Antioch

²⁷During this time some prophets came down from Jerusalem to Antioch. ²⁸One of them, named Agabus, stood up and through the Spirit predicted that a severe famine would spread over the entire Roman world. (This happened during the reign of Claudius.) ²⁹The disciples, as each one was able, decided to provide help for the brothers and sisters living in Judea. ³⁰This they did, sending their gift to the elders by Barnabas and Saul.

ACTS 15:1–12

Certain people came down from Judea to Antioch and were teaching the believers: "Unless you are circumcised, according to the custom taught by Moses, you cannot be saved." ²This brought Paul and Barnabas into sharp dispute and debate with them. So Paul and Barnabas were appointed, along with some other believers, to go up to Jerusalem to see the apostles and elders about this question. ³The church sent them on their way, and as they traveled through Phoenicia and Samaria, they told how the Gentiles had been converted. This news made all the believers very glad. ⁴When they came to Jerusalem, they were welcomed by the church and the apostles and elders, to whom they reported everything God had done through them.

⁵Then some of the believers who belonged to the party of the Pharisees stood up and said, "The Gentiles must be circumcised and required to keep the law of Moses."

⁶The apostles and elders met to consider this question. ⁷After much discussion, Peter got up and addressed them: "Brothers, you know that some time ago God made a choice among you that the Gentiles might hear from my lips the message of the gospel and believe. ⁸God, who knows the heart, showed that he accepted them by giving the Holy Spirit to them, just as he did to us. ⁹He did not discriminate between us and them, for he purified their hearts by faith. ¹⁰Now then, why do you try to test God by putting on the necks of Gentiles a yoke that neither we nor our ancestors

have been able to bear? ¹¹No! We believe it is through the grace of our Lord Jesus that we are saved, just as they are."

¹²The whole assembly became silent as they listened to Barnabas and Paul telling about the signs and wonders God had done among the Gentiles through them.

REFLECTION

In the last session, we saw the Spirit stretch Peter and some Jews to welcome Gentiles into the Christian community. In this session, we read the change that took effect in Antioch and how it eventually changed the whole church. In verse nineteen, we read that when preaching began in Antioch, it was to only Jews. However, some people told the Gentiles about Jesus, and a great number of them became believers. In Jerusalem, the main Christian community heard about this and sent Barnabas to oversee how this was going to work out.

It says Barnabas was "a good man, filled with the Holy Spirit and faith" (verse twenty-four). That explains why he was sent. The Holy Spirit would have to guide this new movement in the church and heal the past discord between Jews and Gentiles. This would take a miracle. In his wisdom, Barnabas went and found Saul now known as Paul, who he knew could speak to the Gentiles. Paul's education and life story made him a perfect instrument for God to use in order to accomplish this task. Together they watched the Holy Spirit break down barriers and heal prejudices. They would witness the transforming power of the Holy Spirit molding very different people into a unified community. It was an unprecedented miracle.

Barnabas is an example of a great Christian leader. When he arrived in Antioch, he witnessed Jews and Gentiles together. This would have gone against his Jewish sensitivities, but it says he saw this as the grace of God. He had eyes that could see beyond his own story. He rejoiced and encouraged the community to remain faithful to Jesus. Faithfully following Jesus' way was the unifying bond in this new "mixed" community.

In chapter fifteen, we read how Barnabas and Paul traveled to Jerusalem to explain this new phenomenon to the larger church. With the testimony of Peter and their own testimony of what God was doing in Antioch, they convinced the larger church to welcome Gentiles. This is a great testament of Spirit-led leaders. There would be challenges as they faced table fellowship, but the Holy Spirit brought about an amazing unity with time.

Interestingly, when the Jews in Jerusalem faced a famine (11:27–30), both Jews and Gentiles who did not know the people in Jerusalem set aside money to be taken to them. They would have had to overcome many relational barriers to put their contribution in that collection. I have seen the Holy Spirit overcome considerable obstacles. Once at a gathering of charismatic Christian leaders from all over the world, I heard a Catholic priest talk about the prayer group he led in Ireland. That was at the time when there was intense fighting going on there between Protestants and Catholics. He spoke of how the Holy Spirit broke down walls and healed hearts to such a degree that their prayer group included people from both sides of that on-going fight. The differences melted in the fire of the Holy Spirit. When he finished his talk, he went over and embraced the Protestant pastor from that same area. The "impossible" can happen when the Spirit of God is leading.

QUESTIONS FOR REFLECTION/DISCUSSION

1. How has the testimony of someone brought you to believe in Jesus and his healing mission?

2. What inner healing do you think had to happen for Jews and Gentiles to get along and affirm each other?

3. Barnabas and Paul met resistance in Jerusalem about their ministry. How do you think they stood their ground and brought about change?

4. What practices would have had to change for Jews and Gentiles to eat together? How might we change certain language and practices to welcome new people into our church community?

5. What would make a Gentile in Antioch give money to feed a Jew in Jerusalem? What greater thing was going on?

6. What insight about living the Christian life did you receive from this session?

TIME OF PRAYER WITH EACH OTHER

PRACTICAL APPLICATION

Talk with your church leaders about rituals and language that may not be inviting to guests.

SESSION 14

Healings in Lystra

PRAYER

READ ACTS 14:1-11

At Iconium Paul and Barnabas went as usual into the Jewish synagogue. There they spoke so effectively that a great number of Jews and Greeks believed. ²But the Jews who refused to believe stirred up the other Gentiles and poisoned their minds against the brothers. ³So Paul and Barnabas spent considerable time there, speaking boldly for the Lord, who confirmed the message of his grace by enabling them to perform signs and wonders. ⁴The people of the city were divided; some sided with the Jews, others with the apostles. ⁵There was a plot afoot among both Gentiles and Jews, together with their leaders, to mistreat them and stone them. ⁶But they found out about it and fled to the Lycaonian cities of Lystra and Derbe and to the surrounding country, ⁷where they continued to preach the gospel.

⁸In Lystra there sat a man who was lame. He had been that way from birth and had never walked. ⁹He listened to Paul as he was speaking. Paul looked directly at him, saw that he had faith to

be healed [10]and called out, "Stand up on your feet!" At that, the man jumped up and began to walk.

[11]When the crowd saw what Paul had done, they shouted in the Lycaonian language, "The gods have come down to us in human form!"

ACTS 14:14-23

[14]But when the apostles Barnabas and Paul heard of this, they tore their clothes and rushed out into the crowd, shouting: [15]"Friends, why are you doing this? We too are only human, like you. We are bringing you good news, telling you to turn from these worthless things to the living God, who made the heavens and the earth and the sea and everything in them. [16]In the past, he let all nations go their own way. [17]Yet he has not left himself without testimony: He has shown kindness by giving you rain from heaven and crops in their seasons; he provides you with plenty of food and fills your hearts with joy." [18]Even with these words, they had difficulty keeping the crowd from sacrificing to them.

[19]Then some Jews came from Antioch and Iconium and won the crowd over. They stoned Paul and dragged him outside the city, thinking he was dead. [20]But after the disciples had gathered around him, he got up and went back into the city. The next day he and Barnabas left for Derbe.

[21]They preached the gospel in that city and won a large number of disciples. Then they returned to Lystra, Iconium and Antioch, [22]strengthening the disciples and encouraging them to remain true to the faith. "We must go through many hardships to enter the kingdom of God," they said. [23]Paul and Barnabas appointed elders for them in each church and, with prayer and fasting, committed them to the Lord, in whom they had put their trust.

Healings in Lystra

REFLECTION

This section not only shows us the challenges Paul and Barnabas faced in proclaiming the message of Jesus but also demonstrates the power of the Holy Spirit to heal and change lives. They continued their mission to both Jews and Gentiles, but they faced constant resistance. Preaching Jesus' message in every culture has been met with resistance. It is tempting to alter the message to fit the culture. It is a challenge to study Jesus' teaching, learn his ways, and listen continually to his voice as we preach, teach, and heal in his name. Staying faithful to Jesus' message takes courage and persistent listening. Paul and Barnabas stayed faithful to Jesus' teaching and moved on to those who would receive it, "filled with joy and the Holy Spirit."

In Lystra Paul came upon a man lame from birth. Seeing his faith, Paul gave a word of command, "Stand up on your feet." The man was instantly healed. As we have seen in earlier passages, such a confident word comes only through a person walking closely in the Spirit of God. It must be God's word and not from human origin. The healing story is short. It is a simple demonstration of the power available to Christians filled with the Holy Spirit.

In verse fifteen, we read about Paul's humility and awareness that whatever miraculous power is seen through his ministry comes from God and is meant to lead people into a life-giving relationship with God. He resisted fame and wealth from his ministry. He was serving the Master.

While Paul's ministry was life-giving to some, others were jealous and tried to stop him. They stoned him and dragged him outside the town, leaving him for dead. Here we witness the healing power flowing through Paul's disciples as they gathered around him and prayed. Soon Paul was healed. With Spirit-led courage, he went right back into that town and continued his ministry. Sometimes we can get "stoned" by people who do not like our preaching of Jesus' message. It is a great blessing to have a team who stand with us and pray for us. I am grateful to the many "disciples" who have stood by me through the years as I taught the message of Jesus. It is a treasure to have a healing community.

Before Paul and Barnabas left these Galatian towns, they gave their disciples reassurances and encouragement to persevere in the faith. "With prayer and fasting," they selected and commissioned leaders to continue the ministry they had begun. They passed on the empowerment of the Holy Spirit to those who could guide these new-found communities. They demonstrated the important qualities of Spirit-led leaders.

QUESTIONS FOR REFLECTION/DISCUSSION

1. How does jealousy today harm or alter the mission of Jesus?

2. What do you think the disciples of Paul felt like when their leader was dead? What did they do?

3. If you had lived in these Galatian towns, how would you have responded to the preaching of Paul and Barnabas?

4. How do you choose leaders in your community? Does it involve prayer and fasting and the guidance of the Holy Spirit?

5. What leadership qualities evident in Acts of the Apostles do you see in your Christian leaders?

Healings in Lystra

TIME OF PRAYER WITH EACH OTHER

PRACTICAL APPLICATION

Affirm a quality in one of your Christian leaders that matches the qualities found in these Scriptures.

Session 15

Healings in Philippi

PRAYER

READ ACTS 16:13-38

¹³On the Sabbath we went outside the city gate to the river, where we expected to find a place of prayer. We sat down and began to speak to the women who had gathered there. ¹⁴One of those listening was a woman from the city of Thyatira named Lydia, a dealer in purple cloth. She was a worshiper of God. The Lord opened her heart to respond to Paul's message. ¹⁵When she and the members of her household were baptized, she invited us to her home. "If you consider me a believer in the Lord," she said, "come and stay at my house." And she persuaded us.

¹⁶Once when we were going to the place of prayer, we were met by a female slave who had a spirit by which she predicted the future. She earned a great deal of money for her owners by fortune-telling. ¹⁷She followed Paul and the rest of us, shouting, "These men are servants of the Most High God, who are telling you the way to be saved." ¹⁸She kept this up for many days. Finally, Paul became so annoyed that he turned around and said to the

Healings in Philippi

spirit, "In the name of Jesus Christ I command you to come out of her!" At that moment the spirit left her.

¹⁹When her owners realized that their hope of making money was gone, they seized Paul and Silas and dragged them into the marketplace to face the authorities. ²⁰They brought them before the magistrates and said, "These men are Jews, and are throwing our city into an uproar ²¹by advocating customs unlawful for us Romans to accept or practice."

²²The crowd joined in the attack against Paul and Silas, and the magistrates ordered them to be stripped and beaten with rods. ²³After they had been severely flogged, they were thrown into prison, and the jailer was commanded to guard them carefully. ²⁴When he received these orders, he put them in the inner cell and fastened their feet in the stocks.

²⁵About midnight Paul and Silas were praying and singing hymns to God, and the other prisoners were listening to them. ²⁶Suddenly there was such a violent earthquake that the foundations of the prison were shaken. At once all the prison doors flew open, and everyone's chains came loose. ²⁷The jailer woke up, and when he saw the prison doors open, he drew his sword and was about to kill himself because he thought the prisoners had escaped. ²⁸But Paul shouted, "Don't harm yourself! We are all here!"

²⁹The jailer called for lights, rushed in and fell trembling before Paul and Silas. ³⁰He then brought them out and asked, "Sirs, what must I do to be saved?"

³¹They replied, "Believe in the Lord Jesus, and you will be saved—you and your household." ³²Then they spoke the word of the Lord to him and to all the others in his house. ³³At that hour of the night the jailer took them and washed their wounds; then immediately he and all his household were baptized. ³⁴The jailer brought them into his house and set a meal before them; he was filled with joy because he had come to believe in God—he and his whole household.

³⁵When it was daylight, the magistrates sent their officers to the jailer with the order: "Release those men." ³⁶The jailer told

Paul, "The magistrates have ordered that you and Silas be released. Now you can leave. Go in peace."

³⁷But Paul said to the officers: "They beat us publicly without a trial, even though we are Roman citizens, and threw us into prison. And now do they want to get rid of us quietly? No! Let them come themselves and escort us out."

³⁸The officers reported this to the magistrates, and when they heard that Paul and Silas were Roman citizens, they were alarmed. ³⁹They came to appease them and escorted them from the prison, requesting them to leave the city. ⁴⁰After Paul and Silas came out of the prison, they went to Lydia's house, where they met with the brothers and sisters and encouraged them. Then they left.

REFLECTION

As we read these accounts of Paul's travels, it seems clear that he did not travel around randomly but waited and listened to the direction of the Holy Spirit. Jesus' Spirit guided his way. Paul's protection was being in the tracks that Jesus laid out for him. No matter where Jesus took him, there was always ministry to be done.

In Philippi, we read of Paul going out to pray, but he was also open to the next opportunity for ministry in Jesus' name. He preached to Lydia and her household and baptized all of them. A girl possessed by a spirit followed him, shouting about who he and his followers were. After several days, he commanded the spirit to leave, and immediately the girl was freed from the clairvoyant spirit and her slavery. That spirit was no match for the power of the Holy Spirit. A girl was set free, but her masters lost some of their profit. For this act of kindness, Paul and Silas were flogged and put in prison, with their feet chained to a stake.

It has always been inspiring to me what Paul and Silas did in prison. They prayed and sang hymns to God. They intentionally stayed in the presence of God. I have heard testimonies of healings happening during pure worship when people feel the loving presence of God surrounding them. It was customary at our church to sing songs of praise for fifteen minutes as people gathered before

Healings in Philippi

the Communion service. We sang many heart songs in which the words are addressed to Jesus and express our love for him. These songs pulled people into prayer and immersed them in the holy love of God. Once after worship, a woman said that she had tremendous pain in her leg when she came to church, but her pain healed during our singing. In my ministry, I celebrated many inner healing services, and often the music would enable people to feel God's personal love. It gave them the environment to release their inner pain and experience healing.

Paul and Silas' worship ministered to the other inmates and broke open the doors of the prison. This caused the jailer to think he had failed. He tried to kill himself before he would be killed by his superior. Paul stopped him and offered him a new way of living. The singing and subsequent miracle of freedom caused the jailer to ask the important question, "What must I do to be saved?" Paul then had the opportunity to teach and baptize the jailer and his whole family. Paul's ability to consistently manifest the love of Jesus, even in prison, allowed him to change numerous lives. He had an interior power given to him by the Holy Spirit. He stayed faithfully committed to the mission of Jesus despite other people's responses. He trusted the direction of the Holy Spirit, even when it was difficult. Verse thirty-four tells us that his ministry brought joy to a whole family. Seeing that joy and their new faith must have continued to motivate Paul.

The last five verses of this section are quite informative. They reveal an interesting fact. They tell us that if Paul had spoken up, he would not have had to get beaten with a rod and spend the night in prison. He was a Roman citizen. We might wonder what he was thinking that he did not speak up. My guess is that he was not thinking but rather listening, listening to the Holy Spirit. His silence cost him some severe pain, but having a chance to evangelize in jail and bring a family to faith was an opportunity that pleased his Master, and it brought joy to his heart.

Healing Miracles in Acts of the Apostles

QUESTIONS FOR REFLECTION/DISCUSSION

1. What would it be like if we asked God every morning, "What do you want me to be doing today?" How would it change the way we are attentive to ministry opportunities?

2. How do you set aside a place and time for prayer every day? How does it empower you?

3. Paul was accused of "disturbing the peace" with his preaching. Has your proclaiming of the saving and healing power of Jesus ever "disturbed" someone? What did you do?

4. Have you ever experienced or witnessed the healing power of pure worship? Share.

5. If someone asked you, "What must I do to be saved," what would you tell them?

6. What insight about living the Christian life did you receive from this session?

TIME OF PRAYER WITH EACH OTHER

PRACTICAL APPLICATION

Invite someone to a place where they could experience heart songs sung to God.

SESSION 16

Miracles in Ephesus

PRAYER

READ ACTS 19:1-20

While Apollos was at Corinth, Paul took the road through the interior and arrived at Ephesus. There he found some disciples ²and asked them, "Did you receive the Holy Spirit when you believed?"

They answered, "No, we have not even heard that there is a Holy Spirit."

³So Paul asked, "Then what baptism did you receive?"

"John's baptism," they replied.

⁴Paul said, "John's baptism was a baptism of repentance. He told the people to believe in the one coming after him, that is, in Jesus." ⁵On hearing this, they were baptized in the name of the Lord Jesus. ⁶When Paul placed his hands on them, the Holy Spirit came on them, and they spoke in tongues and prophesied. ⁷There were about twelve men in all.

⁸Paul entered the synagogue and spoke boldly there for three months, arguing persuasively about the kingdom of God. ⁹But some of them became obstinate; they refused to believe and publicly maligned the Way. So Paul left them. He took the disciples

Miracles in Ephesus

with him and had discussions daily in the lecture hall of Tyrannus. ¹⁰This went on for two years, so that all the Jews and Greeks who lived in the province of Asia heard the word of the Lord.

¹¹God did extraordinary miracles through Paul, ¹²so that even handkerchiefs and aprons that had touched him were taken to the sick, and their illnesses were cured and the evil spirits left them.

¹³Some Jews who went around driving out evil spirits tried to invoke the name of the Lord Jesus over those who were demon-possessed. They would say, "In the name of the Jesus whom Paul preaches, I command you to come out." ¹⁴Seven sons of Sceva, a Jewish chief priest, were doing this. ¹⁵One day the evil spirit answered them, "Jesus I know, and Paul I know about, but who are you?" ¹⁶Then the man who had the evil spirit jumped on them and overpowered them all. He gave them such a beating that they ran out of the house naked and bleeding.

¹⁷When this became known to the Jews and Greeks living in Ephesus, they were all seized with fear, and the name of the Lord Jesus was held in high honor. ¹⁸Many of those who believed now came and openly confessed what they had done. ¹⁹A number who had practiced sorcery brought their scrolls together and burned them publicly. When they calculated the value of the scrolls, the total came to fifty thousand drachmas. ²⁰In this way the word of the Lord spread widely and grew in power.

REFLECTION

When Paul arrived in Ephesus, he found an interesting situation. There were believers in that city, but they had not heard of the Holy Spirit. They had only been baptized with the baptism of John. Paul then taught them about Jesus and baptized them in the name of Jesus. After that, he laid hands on them, and they received a second anointing of the Holy Spirit, which enabled them to speak in tongues and prophesy. Each community needed specific ministry to experience the fullness of the Holy Spirit and the gifts of the Spirit. Those gifts were given not for the person's benefit, but to carry out Jesus' mission. When Christians take time to receive those gifts, more transforming ministry goes on in that community.

The reading goes on to say that God worked "extraordinary miracles" at the hands of Paul. These even happened when people touched handkerchiefs and cloths that had touched him. The healing and freeing power of God's love knows no limits. The recording of these miracles has inspired prayer cloths and blankets that continue to the present. In our healing community, we would pray God's love on the blankets. People would then take them to those who needed healing. A woman of our community shared one such blanket with another woman in a nursing home. As the woman wrapped herself in the blanket, all her pain went away. She felt God's healing love.

Verses 13–17 speak of the stark reality that if anyone is going to try to cast out evil, they had better be connected to the divine power of God. We do not have to fear taking authority over evil spirits; we only need to know that it is God's authority. Healings and deliverances only happen through people who are filled with the Holy Spirit and willing to use the gifts of the Spirit to bring wholeness to others. Once we are filled with the anointing of the Holy Spirit, we can confidently bind any spirit and send it to Jesus. Christian Healing Ministries has some very good videos and books on deliverance available at *www.christianhealingmin.org*. The deliverance ministry takes some training, but it is powerful and necessary in some instances.

The last verses tell us that part of committing to a relationship with Jesus, and opening to the power of the Holy Spirit, is to empty oneself and turn away from practices and materials that are not in keeping with Jesus' teaching. Freeing ourselves of past wrongs or involvements may include taking moral inventory and confessing as it did in Ephesus. Throwing away books or objects can help cleanse our environment of negative energy or evil forces and free us to rest in the peace of Jesus every day. Also, reading the words of Jesus in scripture or listening to scripture-based songs can fill us with the positive energy of his presence. Some people find that having pictures or images of Jesus can allow them to feel his presence in a deeper way. We use whatever enriches our spiritual walk with him.

QUESTIONS FOR REFLECTION/DISCUSSION

1. Do you know people who believe in Jesus but have never experienced the anointing of the Holy Spirit? How might you invite them to something more?

2. Have you ever experienced any of the gifts of the Holy Spirit as described by St. Paul in 1 Cor 12:4–11? Have you seen them used by others? Share.

3. What do you think it feels like to have a prayer blanket wrapped around you? Would you give one to someone who is ill?

4. Have you ever thrown away books and materials that are incongruous with the teachings of Jesus? If not, what effect do you think it would have?

5. Have you ever received inner healing prayer for memories of traumatic experiences that keep you from feeling the full power of the Holy Spirit? If not, what effect do you think it would have?

TIME OF PRAYER WITH EACH OTHER

PRACTICAL APPLICATION

Look through your house and get rid of any things that hamper your relationship with Jesus. Fill the spaces with things that enrich that relationship.

SESSION 17

The Raising of Eutychus

PRAYER

READ ACTS 20:7-12

⁷On the first day of the week we came together to break bread. Paul spoke to the people and, because he intended to leave the next day, kept on talking until midnight. ⁸There were many lamps in the upstairs room where we were meeting. ⁹Seated in a window was a young man named Eutychus, who was sinking into a deep sleep as Paul talked on and on. When he was sound asleep, he fell to the ground from the third story and was picked up dead. ¹⁰Paul went down, threw himself on the young man and put his arms around him. "Don't be alarmed," he said. "He's alive!" ¹¹Then he went upstairs again and broke bread and ate. After talking until daylight, he left. ¹²The people took the young man home alive and were greatly comforted.

ACTS 20:17-24

¹⁷From Miletus, Paul sent to Ephesus for the elders of the church. ¹⁸When they arrived, he said to them: "You know how I lived the

whole time I was with you, from the first day I came into the province of Asia. ¹⁹I served the Lord with great humility and with tears and in the midst of severe testing by the plots of my Jewish opponents. ²⁰You know that I have not hesitated to preach anything that would be helpful to you but have taught you publicly and from house to house. ²¹I have declared to both Jews and Greeks that they must turn to God in repentance and have faith in our Lord Jesus.

²²"And now, compelled by the Spirit, I am going to Jerusalem, not knowing what will happen to me there. ²³I only know that in every city the Holy Spirit warns me that prison and hardships are facing me. ²⁴However, I consider my life worth nothing to me; my only aim is to finish the race and complete the task the Lord Jesus has given me—the task of testifying to the good news of God's grace.

ACTS 20:28-32

²⁸Keep watch over yourselves and all the flock of which the Holy Spirit has made you overseers. Be shepherds of the church of God, which he bought with his own blood. ²⁹I know that after I leave, savage wolves will come in among you and will not spare the flock. ³⁰Even from your own number men will arise and distort the truth in order to draw away disciples after them. ³¹So be on your guard! Remember that for three years I never stopped warning each of you night and day with tears.

³²"Now I commit you to God and to the word of his grace, which can build you up and give you an inheritance among all those who are sanctified.

ACTS 20:36-38

³⁶When Paul had finished speaking, he knelt down with all of them and prayed. ³⁷They all wept as they embraced him and kissed him. ³⁸What grieved them most was his statement that they would never see his face again. Then they accompanied him to the ship.

The Raising of Eutychus

REFLECTION

A reader might not notice, but verse seven tells us of the early community's practice of the gathering for the Eucharist or Communion on every Sunday. This important practice gave people a chance to recommit their lives to Jesus and the community. Communities from various cities and towns could feel the support and unity of celebrating the Breaking of Bread as one on that day. Later sources tell us that if a person missed this celebration three times in a row, they would have to be re-admitted to the community. That shows the significance of this event. They made an adult commitment of their life to Jesus at their baptism, and weekly Eucharist was the time they renewed that commitment of their body and blood to Jesus. I grew up in a tradition which taught me that a person had to go to Eucharist every Sunday. It was an obligation. Once I experienced the infusion of the Holy Spirit, Jesus became a treasured friend. From then on, I "had" to go to Eucharist every Sunday to celebrate a meal with my friend and recommit my body and blood to him as he committed his to me. I continue to start each week with that friendship meal. He fills and refreshes me for that week's mission.

We read further about Eutychus sitting on the window sill listening to Paul speak. He fell asleep and fell from the third story window sill and died. It must have been alarming for the family, but for Paul, it was an opportunity to manifest the life-giving power of the risen Jesus. Paul demonstrated his faith in the power of God as he prayed the life of Jesus back into the boy, who went home with those present. The story is short but powerful. Paul's life in the Spirit gave him access to an amazing energy source.

The rest of this section gives us a glimpse into the heart of Paul. He was being led by the Holy Spirit to go back to Jerusalem, but that same Spirit warned of hardship there. Paul expresses his vision of life. He says, "I put no value on my life if only I can finish my race and complete the service to which I have been assigned by the Lord Jesus, bearing witness to the gospel of God's grace." He was all in, totally committed to Jesus. It is a miracle that this one-time persecutor of Christians could fall so deeply in love with his Master. No matter what our past story is, by God's grace, we can live a life immersed in the presence of the Holy Spirit. Divine power has no limits.

Paul gives some final words to the leaders in Miletus. He warns them to stay empowered by the Spirit and to shepherd the community with care. They would have to ward off the "wolves" who would come perverting the truth of the gospel. One of the primary roles of those early Christian leaders was to guard and preserve the truth of the gospel. It is equally important today, with so many temptations to stray from what Jesus taught. The wisdom of the Spirit is crucial to sort out the truth, and the power of the Spirit is needed to proclaim it with boldness.

Following several directives, we read of the tearful goodbyes. When people are connected in the power of the Holy Spirit, the relationships take on a new depth. This is what Paul in his letters calls, relating "in the Lord." The joy of those relationships is that they are eternal.

QUESTIONS FOR REFLECTION/DISCUSSION

1. How important is weekly Communion to you? Do you have a worshipping community where you can get refreshed in the Spirit each week?

2. What do you think Eutychus felt like after he was raised up? How do you think his life changed?

3. Paul never backed away from preaching the message of Jesus. Have you ever heard of others who backed away from

The Raising of Eutychus

speaking the message of Jesus because of pressure from the culture? Has it ever happened to you?

4. Which of Paul's final words to the community at Miletus do you find most inspiring?

5. What attributes of Paul do you find most attractive? Do you see those attributes in yourself or others?

TIME OF PRAYER WITH EACH OTHER

PRACTICAL APPLICATION

Next time you celebrate Communion, feel the deep love Jesus has for you.

SESSION 18

Healings in Malta

PRAYER

READ ACTS 27:22-24

²²But now I urge you to keep up your courage, because not one of you will be lost; only the ship will be destroyed. ²³Last night an angel of the God to whom I belong and whom I serve stood beside me ²⁴and said, 'Do not be afraid, Paul. You must stand trial before Caesar; and God has graciously given you the lives of all who sail with you.'

ACTS 27:41-44

⁴¹But the ship struck a sandbar and ran aground. The bow stuck fast and would not move, and the stern was broken to pieces by the pounding of the surf.
⁴²The soldiers planned to kill the prisoners to prevent any of them from swimming away and escaping. ⁴³But the centurion wanted to spare Paul's life and kept them from carrying out their plan. He ordered those who could swim to jump overboard first

and get to land. ⁴⁴The rest were to get there on planks or on other pieces of the ship. In this way everyone reached land safely.

ACTS 28:1-10

Once safely on shore, we found out that the island was called Malta. ²The islanders showed us unusual kindness. They built a fire and welcomed us all because it was raining and cold. ³Paul gathered a pile of brushwood and, as he put it on the fire, a viper, driven out by the heat, fastened itself on his hand. ⁴When the islanders saw the snake hanging from his hand, they said to each other, "This man must be a murderer; for though he escaped from the sea, the goddess Justice has not allowed him to live." ⁵But Paul shook the snake off into the fire and suffered no ill effects. ⁶The people expected him to swell up or suddenly fall dead; but after waiting a long time and seeing nothing unusual happen to him, they changed their minds and said he was a god.

⁷There was an estate nearby that belonged to Publius, the chief official of the island. He welcomed us to his home and showed us generous hospitality for three days. ⁸His father was sick in bed, suffering from fever and dysentery. Paul went in to see him and, after prayer, placed his hands on him and healed him. ⁹When this had happened, the rest of the sick on the island came and were cured. ¹⁰They honored us in many ways; and when we were ready to sail, they furnished us with the supplies we needed.

REFLECTION

We pick up this story with Paul on a ship headed for Rome but now facing a shipwreck from a storm. Again, we read how Paul is guided by God, who assured him not to be afraid, for he would be safe. The months before I was to be ordained, I felt the fear of having to preach each Sunday and lead a congregation. I would often sing the words of a song, "Be not afraid, I go before you. Come follow me, and I will give you rest." Those words of Jesus have sustained me through many fearful events and continue to keep me at peace as I step into the next mission Jesus has for me.

The scripture tells us that the ship in this story was wrecked, but everyone on board made it safely to Malta, just as God had promised. Paul was under the protection of the Creator, and he was destined to preach in Rome. Paul would suffer much, but Jesus protected him from death until his "race" was over.

It seems that tragedy strikes when Paul gets bitten by a poisonous snake, but he had a powerful "immune system." The people expected him to die, but God had greater plans. His healing opened the door for him to heal many people on that island. A possible tragedy became an opportunity for a divine display of power. The father of the island leader was ill, and as Paul was used to doing, he prayed with him, and he man was healed. Because of that healing, the rest of the sick on the island came, and it says, "they too were healed." For those people, this was an amazing miracle. For Paul, it was a constant testimony that the risen Jesus was alive.

Several years ago, we spent five days on the island of Malta teaching leaders about the healing power of Jesus. They had a very vibrant faith, and they were eager to learn more about Jesus. It was as if the spirit of Jesus that Paul brought was still present there. At the final healing service, we saw many miracles occur. There was an excitement, anticipation, and a desire to receive all that God was doing. It was a hard place to leave. That was where the woman whose leg was healed came walking and jumping through the airport, praising God for her healing.

The power of the Holy Spirit has been seen throughout this whole journey into Acts of the Apostles. It never faded away. The good news is that it is still present on earth today, made visible through all who open themselves to the full power of that Spirit. It is miraculous. It is beyond rational explanation. It simply is. It is part of the gospel message. Jesus said he came to bring the fullness of life, and he sent his Spirit to continue his mission. His ministry and that of his first followers demonstrated that healing was a significant part of their life. We are left to carry on this miraculous story. Through our hands, our feet, our mouths, our "yeses," our commitment, our openness to the Holy Spirit, we bring the message of Jesus into the world today. The miracles continue to happen.

QUESTIONS FOR REFLECTION/DISCUSSION

1. Have you ever been in a scary situation and heard Jesus say, "Do not be afraid, I am with you." Share.

2. What do you think the centurion on the ship saw in Paul that he was anxious to save him?

3. After Paul did not die from the snake bite, they began to say he was a god. How is humility an important part of the healing ministry?

4. What do you think all the island people felt when they saw so many healings?

5. How has this series on miracles in Acts of the Apostles helped you better understand the healing ministry and the power of the Holy Spirit? With whom could you share this message?

TIME OF PRAYER WITH EACH OTHER

PRACTICAL APPLICATION

Go and live your Christian life to the fullest

Recommmended Reading

Crowe, Jerome. *The Acts*. Delaware: Michael Glazier, 1979. (This book offers a good theological background to Acts of the Apostles.)

Feider, Paul. *Resting in the Heart*. Oregon: Wipf and Stock, 2001. (This book offers simple, clear steps, along with scriptural reflections, to assist people in receiving physical and inner healing.)

Johnson, Bill. *When Heaven Invades Earth*. Pennsylvania: Destiny Image, 2005. (A dynamic presentation of how to bring the power of heaven to the world today through the "special forces" given to us by the Holy Spirit.)

Kelsey, Morton. *Healing and Christianity*. New York: Harper and Row, 1973. (A book that gives an excellent, complete history of the Christian healing ministry.)

MacNutt, Francis. *The Healing Reawakening*. Michigan: Chosen Books, 2005 (A unique account of how Jesus' healing ministry has survived through the centuries of Christianity and is viable today.)

McBride, Alfred. *The Gospel of the Holy Spirit*. New York: Hawthorn Books, 1975. (A compelling presentation of the movement of the Holy Spirit in the apostolic church.)

Miller, Craig. *Breaking Emotional Barriers to Healing*. Pennsylvania: Whitaker House, 2018. (This book shows the connection between physical illness and emotional woundedness with data and inspiring stories.)

www.ingramcontent.com/pod-product-compliance
Lightning Source LLC
Chambersburg PA
CBHW070311100426
42743CB00011B/2435